AF450749

Saved By Love

A Story Of London Streets

by

Emma Leslie

Saved By Love
A Story Of London Streets
by Emma Leslie

Copyright © 2024

All Rights reserved.

No part of this publication may be reproduced,
stored in a retrieval system, or transmitted in any
form or by any means, electronic, mechanical,
photocopying or Otherwise, without the written
permission of the publisher.
The author/editor asserts the moral right to
be identified as the author/editor of this work.

ISBN: 978-93-69073-24-5

Published by

DOUBLE 9 BOOKS

2/13-B, Ansari Road
Daryaganj, New Delhi – 110002
info@double9books.com
www.double9books.com
Tel. 011-40042856

This book is under public domain

ABOUT THE AUTHOR

Emma Leslie, a prolific author of the 19th century, crafted the captivating masterpiece "Hayslope Grange: A Tale of the Civil War." Set against the backdrop of the tumultuous Civil War era, Leslie's novel intricately weaves together the lives of its characters amidst the chaos and upheaval of the times. With vivid prose and compelling storytelling, Leslie transports readers to the heart of Hayslope Grange, where the echoes of battle reverberate and the bonds of family and loyalty are tested. Through the eyes of her characters, Leslie offers a poignant exploration of love, loss, and resilience in the face of adversity. Against the backdrop of war, secrets are revealed, alliances forged, and sacrifices made, as the characters navigate the turbulent currents of history. As a master storyteller, Emma Leslie's "Hayslope Grange" stands as a timeless testament to her talent for capturing the human experience amidst the backdrop of historical events. With its richly drawn characters and gripping narrative, this masterpiece continues to captivate readers, offering a compelling glimpse into the complexities of life during the Civil War era.

CONTENTS

CHAPTER I
ALL ALONE IN LONDON

THERE are some places in London where King Dirt holds a carnival all the year round—narrow back streets, where the tall houses, almost meeting at the top, shut out every gleam of sunlight, except during the longest and hottest days of summer; and then only a narrow rift of golden glory lights up a strip in the centre, and makes the shady corners look more dark and desolate than ever.

In one of the shadowed nooks of such a street sat a little girl, her head leaning against the brick wall for a pillow; and you might have thought her fast asleep, but for an occasional sob. She had cried so long that her eyes were swollen and heavy; and even the faint light of Fisher's Lane made them ache so much that she was glad to close them.

No one noticed her for some time, but at length a girl about her own age stopped and looked at her, and at last spoke.

"What's the matter?" she said, touching her shoulder.

With a sob and a start the girl opened her eyes.

"O Elfie, is it you?" she said; and then her tears broke out afresh.

"What is it? Haven't you got anything to eat?" she asked.

"I shall never want to eat anything again," sobbed the other. "O Elfie, mother's dead!"

"Dead, is she?" said Elfie, but looking as though she could not understand why that should cause any one to cry.

"I shall never be happy again, Elfie. O mother, mother, why didn't you take me with you?" wailed the poor little orphan.

"Just because she didn't want you, I guess," said Elfie, but at the same time sitting down to soothe the grief she could not understand. "There, don't cry," she went on in a matter-of-fact tone. "My mother's gone away, but I don't cry after her; not a bit of it; I know better than that, Susie Sanders."

Susie shrank from her companion's touch as she said this, and thought of what her mother had said about making companions of the children in the street, and half regretted having spoken to Elfie. There was a great difference in the two girls, any one could see, though both might be equally poor. Elfie was unmistakably a street child, ragged, dirty, sharp-looking, with bright cunning eyes shining out of a good-tempered-looking face; while Susie, in her patched black frock and tidy pinafore, and timid, shrinking ways, showed unmistakably that, poor as she might be, there had been some one to love and take care of her. Alas for her, poor child! Her only friend in the wide world had died that morning, leaving her alone in the streets of London.

It was the old, old story: a widow striving to work for herself and her only child, and sinking at last beneath the stroke of disease, after giving up one by one every article of furniture, and moving from place to place, until at last she was glad to find a refuge in the garret of one of these gaunt houses, where she had not lived many weeks before God called her to the mansion he had prepared for her.

She had talked to Susie of this, and tried to prepare the child's mind for the coming of the sad trial; but the little girl had hoped that her mother would get better "by-and-by." And so, when at last she woke up that morning and leaned over her mother, and found that she could not speak, nor even return the caresses lavished on her cold lips and brow, she grew frightened at the unwonted stillness, but yet could not think her mother was dead, until some of the neighbours came in and told her so.

Mrs. Sanders had not made friends with her neighbours, and they had thought her proud, because she did not talk to them of her affairs. And so, beyond telling Susie to go to the overseer of the parish, and ask him to send some one to bury her mother, they did not trouble themselves.

Susie had just been on this errand, and had wandered out again into the street to cry there, when Elfie saw her. They had spoken to each other before, but there had not been much acquaintance, for Mrs. Sanders kept her little girl in-doors as much as possible. But Elfie had taken a fancy to Susie, and resolved to befriend her now; so instead of moving away when she was repulsed, she put her bare grimy arms round Susie's neck, and said—

"Tell us all about it, Susie; the boys shan't hit you while I'm here."

To tell "all about it" was just what Susie wanted. No one else had asked about her mother, except the few hard questions put by the overseer, and so she gladly nestled close up to Elfie, and told of her waking that morning to find her mother cold and dead.

A grief like Susie's was quite beyond Elfie's comprehension. Her mother had left her six months before—gone off no one knew where, and no one cared—at least Elfie did not. No one beat her now, she said; and if she was hungry sometimes, it was better to be hungry than bruised, and no one dared to do that now, so that she was rather glad to be left free to do as she pleased. But Susie shook her head very sadly when told she ought to be glad.

"I can't," she said, "though mother told me that God would take care of me when she was gone. I wanted to go with her; and be happy in heaven now."

"And why didn't she take you?" said Elfie, whose ideas about heaven were not at all clear.

"She said I must stay here a bit longer, and do the work God meant me to do."

"What work's that?" asked Elfie.

Susie shook her head. "I don't know, unless it's sewing shirts like mother did," she said.

"Sewing shirts!" repeated Elfie; "People starve at that, and have to sit still too. I'd rather go about and see places, and starve that way than the other," she added, shrugging her shoulders.

"You don't like sewing, then," said Susie. "What do you do, Elfie, to earn money?"

Elfie laughed. "Oh, it ain't much money I earns; but I manage to get something to eat somehow, and that's what you've got to do now, I suppose."

Again the tears came into Susie's eyes. "I don't know what I'm going to do," she said. "Mother told me to read last night about the ravens taking food to Elijah, and she said God would send his angels here to take care of me."

"Then that shows she knew nothing about this place," said Elfie in her hard, matter-of-fact tone. "Angels don't come down Fisher's Lane—at least I never see 'em, and I'm out pretty near all hours, night and day too."

Susie sighed. "I don't think it was quite an angel with white wings mother meant, but somebody who would be kind and take care of me—a lady or gentleman perhaps," she said.

Elfie laughed. "Catch a lady or gentleman coming down here!" she said.

And the idea of such a thing seemed so ridiculous that she burst into a second peal of laughter, until Susie looked offended.

And then she said more gravely, "It's all a mistake, Susie, about the angels or anybody else caring for you. I know all about it, for I've lived in Fisher's Lane ever since I was born, and people have got to take care of themselves, I can tell you."

"But how shall I take care of myself?" asked Susie. "I know there's some money to pay the rent next week, but when that's gone what am I to do?"

"Get some more," said Elfie shortly. "I'll help you," she added.

"Thank you. Will you come home with me and stay to-night? I'm dull by myself," said Susie with a deep sigh.

Her companion joyfully assented, and went off to the market in search of some stale fruit to share with Susie at once. Then they went back together to Susie's home, and, going up the stairs, overheard two of the women talking to the man who had come to see about the funeral.

Susie was too much overcome with grief to pay any attention to what was said; but Elfie had had all her wits sharpened, and she laid her hand on Susie's arm and made her sit down on the stairs, while she listened to the conversation going on just above them.

When they reached the garret, and Elfie had shut the door and glanced round the room, she said, "Look here, Susie, which will you like best;— to stop here and work for yourself, and go out when you like; or have somebody come and shut you up in a horrible place, with high walls like a prison, and make you work there?"

Susie shivered. "Nobody would do that to me," she said, looking across at the bed where her mother lay covered with the sheet, and thinking what she had said of God caring for her.

"But they will, though, if you don't look sharp, for I heard the woman say you'd better go to the work-house," replied Elfie.

She had heard the work-house spoken of very often, but did not know what it was like, or that the life of children there was far less hard than hers. She only knew they were not allowed to run about the streets; and the idea of being shut up in any place was dreadful to Elfie, and must be to everybody else, she thought.

She succeeded in making Susie dread being taken there.

"But what shall I do to pay the rent here?" she asked.

"Well, it would be nice to stop here," said Elfie; "but I manage without paying rent anywhere and that's a saving of money."

"But where do you go to bed?" asked Susie.

"Well, I ain't been to bed in that sort of bed for nearly six months," she said, pointing towards the corner. "I sleep under a cart, or on a heap of straw, or anywhere I can find a nice place; it don't matter much when you're asleep where you are, so long as you're out of the way of the rats."

Susie shook her head. "I shouldn't like that," she said.

"Well, no, I suppose you wouldn't," said Elfie, again looking round the room. "People that's always been used to tables and chairs, and them sort of things, like you've got here, wouldn't like to sleep out under a waggon, I guess."

"How can people do without tables and chairs?" said Susie. "How can they live?"

"Oh, pretty well! Lots of us have to do without them, and other things besides," said Elfie carelessly; "but you couldn't, I suppose, and so we must try to keep these."

"How shall we do it?" asked Susie.

"Well, you can sew shirts, and I can get a job now and then at the market, and sometimes I clean steps for people, and that all brings money. How much do you pay for this little room?" she asked.

"A shilling a week," answered Susie. "Mother's put the shilling away for next week, and she paid the landlord yesterday."

"All right. Have you got any shirts to sew?" asked Elfie.

Susie opened her mother's bundle of work, and took out two that were unfinished.

"I'll finish them and take them home, and ask them to give me some," she said.

Elfie took one and examined it. "Well, I shouldn't know how to put all them bits in the right places," she said.

This was a difficulty that had never struck Susie. She had helped her mother to make these coarse blue shirts—sewing, hemming, and stitching in turn; but she had never put one together entirely by herself. She looked up in a little dismay.

"I don't think I know how to do it either," she said in a tone of perplexity.

But Elfie turned and turned the shirt about, and at last she said, "Look here, Susie; you'll have to keep one of these back when you take the others home, and then we'll find out how they're to be done between us."

Susie began to think Elfie almost as wise as her mother. She seemed to know how to manage everything, and before evening came she began to look up to her as a friend as well as a companion.

Elfie hardly liked sleeping in the room with that long stretch of whiteness at the farther end. She had never seen Susie's mother while living, and would not have raised the sheet now to look at the still, calm face for anything. She would rather have gone out to sleep in one of the holes or corners of the Adelphi arches, even risking an encounter with the rats, than sleep there; but for Susie's sake she determined to stay.

The next morning she persuaded Susie to sit down to her sewing, while she went out to look for something to eat. Meals taken in the ordinary way Elfie had no idea of; she was used to look about the streets for any scraps of food she could pick up, in the same way that a homeless, hungry dog might do, and so it was no hardship for her to go without her breakfast. Susie had often had to wait for it lately—wait all day, feeling faint and hungry, but obliged to sew and stitch on still, that her mother might get the work home in time. She had to do this to-day, and then could not finish all. But she tied up her bundle, leaving the unfinished one out for a pattern; and then put on her bonnet to go forth to tell the sad story to another—that her mother was dead, and would never sew shirts any more.

As the man counted the shirts over, she said, "Please, sir, I've left one at home, it ain't quite finished; but mother—"

"There, there, child, I can't listen to tales about your mother," interrupted the man; "she's always been honest, and I won't grumble about the shirt this time; but it must not occur again. I can't give you so many either this time, trade is getting dull now."

And pushing Susie's bundle towards her, he turned to another workwoman, and Susie went out wishing she had had the courage to say her mother was dead; for she felt as though she was deceiving him, taking this work to do by herself.

As she went back, Elfie met her. "I've got a nice lot of cold potatoes at home," she said, "and a big handful of cherries that I picked up in the market; and I've seen the work-house man, and told him you ain't going with him."

"What did you say?" asked Susie.

"I told him somebody was coming to live here and take care of you. It's just what I mean to do, Susie," she added; "for I like you, and it'll be fair, you see, if I comes to sleep here when it's cold and wet; for it ain't nice out-of-doors then, I can tell you."

So the compact was formed between these two, and they agreed to help each other and live together, if only the neighbours and work-house people would leave them alone.

They need not have troubled themselves very much about this. The neighbours thought they had done enough when they told the man he had better take Susie to the work-house; while he evidently thought the parish need not be troubled, if she had some one to come and live with and take care of her.

And so, after the coffin was taken out and carried to its lowly resting-place, no one troubled himself to visit the little garret, or look after the lonely orphan. Elfie did not stay in-doors much; but whenever she found anything extra nice, she always ran home to share it with Susie, and faithfully brought in every penny she earned, to put into the tin box where the rent money was kept. Susie succeeded in her shirt-making better than she expected; but life was very hard, and she sorely missed her mother, and shed many bitter tears when she thought of her.

CHAPTER II
GETTING A LIVING

AFTER Mrs. Sanders was buried, people seemed to forget all about Susie. The landlord called for his rent, and Susie paid him; which was all he wanted, so he did not trouble himself to inquire whether she was living alone or had any one to take care of her; and Elfie had told her not to say anything about it unless she was asked.

Elfie was rather proud of her new mode of living—having a roof to shelter her at night, a little spot she could call home—and she honestly believed Susie could not get on without her; and the feeling that she had some one to take care of, made her more careful of the things which were placed under her charge in the market.

But in spite of her care, and the extra employment it often brought her, the rent money could only be made up sometimes by Susie going without food the day before, for she could not eat the rubbish and refuse Elfie seemed to enjoy. A breakfast or dinner of raw pea-shells Susie could not eat above once or twice; and the stale fruit that Elfie brought home for her often made her ill, so that if she could not afford to buy a loaf, she often preferred being hungry to the chance of being ill and unable to work.

But the greatest trouble of all to Susie was the different way in which she spent Sunday. She missed her mother more on that day than any other; for poor as Mrs. Sanders had been, she had always contrived to go to church and take Susie with her, until she came to Fisher's Lane, and was unable to go out on account of illness. Elfie, however, had no other idea of Sunday than of a day to play more and eat less; for as there were no steps to clean nor baskets to mind, and very little refuse to be found about the market, she generally lay down to sleep, feeling very hungry on Sunday night.

Susie always folded up her work and put it away early on Saturday, that she might have time to clean the room, just as her mother had done. And so Elfie, finding her companion was not going to do any needlework on Sunday, persuaded her to come out to play; and for the sake of pleasing her Susie went. But the rough, noisy games of Elfie's companions, Susie could not enjoy, and she was glad to sit down in a quiet corner and think of her mother and the bright home she had gone to. Then she thought of their walks to church, and what she heard there, and how grieved her mother would be if she could see her now playing with these children, until she felt strongly inclined to run off to church now if only she knew her way.

She resolved not to go out to play again on Sunday; and when the next came round, she said, "Do you know your way to church, Elfie?"

"To church!" repeated Elfie. "They won't let us play there."

"No, I don't want to play," said Susie, looking down at her shabby frock, and wondering whether that was fit to go to church in. "I want to do as mother did, and she always went to church on Sundays."

Elfie looked puzzled. "Church ain't for poor people like us," she said.

"Oh yes, it is. Mother used to say she could never bear the trouble at all, if she could not go to church and get some help from God for it on Sundays."

"Eh? It's all along of the tables and chairs, and sleeping in beds, I suppose," said Elfie, a little disdainfully.

"Church has nothing to do with tables and chairs," said Susie. "We go there to hear about God and the Lord Jesus Christ."

"Well, there ain't no God for poor people that don't have tables and chairs," said Elfie.

"O Elfie, don't say that; God loves you, and wants you to know and love him."

"What! Wants me to go to church?" asked Elfie.

Susie nodded. "Come with me, will you?" she said eagerly.

Elfie laughed. "Catch me trying it, won't you; and there's a policeman walking up and down in front all the time."

"But the policeman is not there to keep people from going in," said Susie.

"What does he walk up and down there for, then?" asked Elfie quickly.

Susie could not answer this question, but she said, "Well, I know he don't keep people out."

"Not fine people that's got tables and chairs at home. God wants them in there perhaps, and so he gives the police orders to let 'em in. I know all about it, you see," she added triumphantly.

But Susie shook her head. "No, you don't," she said. "God wants us to know and love him—you and me, Elfie."

"I know them police that stands at the door, and that's enough for me," said the girl. "You can go if you like. Church, and tables, and chairs, and eating off plates, and sleeping in beds, is all one, I guess; and them that gets used to it can't do without it. But I can, and I shan't run to the police for that."

But although Elfie would not go with Susie, she willingly consented to show her the way; for she had not been to a church in this neighbourhood, and only knew the road to take the work backwards and forwards. So, after carefully washing her face and brushing her hair, and making herself as tidy as possible, Susie went out, carrying her prayer-book in her pocket-handkerchief, and trying to fancy that her mother was with her still.

Elfie would not come near the church; but after pointing it out, and watching Susie go in, she ran back to play with her companions, wondering all the time what could be going on inside the church to make Susie so anxious to go there. This was her first question when she met her as she came home.

"What do you look at—what do you do," she asked, "when you go to church?"

"We pray and sing, and hear what the minister says," answered Susie.

"What does he say?" asked Elfie.

Susie thought for a minute, and then answered, "Well, he reads out of the Bible, and says, 'Our Father.' You know that, don't you?"

But Elfie shook her head. "Who is 'Our Father'?" she asked.

"God, who lives up in heaven, where mother's gone," answered Susie.

"He's your Father, then, I suppose," said Elfie.

"Yes, and yours too," said Susie quickly.

"No, he ain't; I don't know him," said Elfie, shaking her head with a little sigh.

"But he knows you, Elfie—knows you, and loves you, and wants you to love him."

But Elfie shook her head persistently. "I don't know nothing about him, and nobody ever loved me," she' said.

And to end the conversation, she ran away to finish her game of buttons, while Susie walked quietly home.

She ate a slice of dry bread for her dinner, and saved one for Elfie; and then took her mother's Bible out of the little box, and sat down to read a chapter just as she used to do before her mother died. But the sight of the familiar old book upset all her firmness, and she sat down with it in her lap, and burst into tears. She was still crying when Elfie came rushing in to ask if she would not come out and join their play.

"What's the matter?" she exclaimed when she saw Susie in tears. "Are you so hungry?" she asked—for hunger seemed the only thing worth crying for to Elfie; and then, seeing the slice of bread on the table, and guessing it had been left for her, she put it on the Bible, saying, "You eat it, Susie; I've had some cold potatoes, and I ain't very hungry now."

But Susie put it back into her hands. "No, no, Elfie; you must eat that," she said. "I'm not crying because I'm hungry."

"What is it then?" said Elfie.

Susie looked down at the book lying in her lap. "I was thinking about mother," she said.

"Are you getting tired of living with me?" asked Elfie quickly.

"Oh no; you're very kind. I don't know what I should do without you, Elfie; but I do want my mother," said Susie through her tears.

Elfie looked puzzled. She was beginning to understand that all the mothers in the world were not like hers—that Susie's was not; and she could not understand why Mrs. Sanders had gone away and left her.

"What made her go away?" she asked.

Susie left off crying to look at her companion in surprise. "Don't you know God took her to heaven?" she said.

"Yes, I know, you said that before," answered Elfie impatiently; "but what made him take her?"

"Because he loved her," said Susie.

"But you said just now he loved you; why didn't he take you up there as well?"

"I asked mother about that one day, when she was telling me she should have to go away; but she said she thought God had some work for me to do in the world first before he took me home." And Susie dried her tears, and tried to be brave and choke back her sobs as she spoke.

"What work will you have to do?" asked Elfie, sitting down on the floor close to Susie's stool. Elfie always preferred rolling on the floor to sitting on any kind of seat; and she greatly enjoyed questioning Susie.

"Mother said God would teach me that if I asked him," answered Susie. "I don't know yet what it will be."

"Then why don't you ask him?" said Elfie in her straightforward fashion.

"I do," whispered Susie. "I ask him every night; because I want to do it, and then go home to mother."

"Is that what you do when you kneel down before you get into bed?" asked Elfie.

Susie nodded. "God hears what I say, too," she answered.

"Well, then, why didn't your mother ask him to let her stay and help you to do the work, if she didn't want to go away?" said Elfie sharply.

Susie knew not what to answer. The question puzzled her not a little; and to escape from Elfie's saying any more, she proposed reading a chapter from the Bible.

Elfie had grown tired of playing, and was quite willing to listen. She could not read herself, and was full of wonder that Susie could; and for some time she chattered and questioned so much about this that Susie could not begin; but at last she grew quiet, and Susie turned to her favourite verses in St. Matthew—the story of young children being brought to Jesus.

"That was kind of him to say, 'Let the children come to me,'" said Elfie when Susie paused.

"Yes; the Lord Jesus is always kind," said Susie.

"I wish he was here in London; I'd go to him," said Elfie. "It's nice to have anybody speak kind to you."

"You can go to him, Elfie," said Susie. "The Lord Jesus has gone up to heaven again now; but he'll hear you just as plain as though he was in the room here."

Elfie stared. "You don't think I'm going to believe that, do you?" she said sharply.

"Why not? It's the truth," said Susie.

"Maybe it is for fine folks that wants a lot of things to live, but not for a poor little street girl like me," answered Elfie.

"Why don't you think it's for you, Elfie?" asked her companion.

"Because I know what I am, and I guess he'd soon find out I was street rubbish, as the fine folks call me in the market." And Elfie clenched her fist angrily as she spoke.

"O Elfie, Jesus don't think you're street rubbish!" said Susie. "I think he cares for people all the more when he knows they're poor, because he was a poor man himself once."

"A poor man!" exclaimed Elfie. "Why, you said he was God's Son, and all the world was his."

"So it is; but when he came down here, the people wouldn't believe he was God's Son, and so he lived like a poor man—as poor as you and I, I think, Elfie."

But Elfie shook her head. "I'm street rubbish, but you ain't," she said.

"I found a verse about it," said Susie, "where Jesus says how poor he was—'The foxes have holes, and the birds of the air have nests, but the Son of man hath not where to lay his head.' There; that means Jesus had no home or comfortable bed, he was so poor," said Susie.

Elfie sat looking at her in dumb surprise.

"He was just as poor as me," she said. "Why didn't he go away, and leave the people, if he was God's Son?"

"Because he loved them, and he wanted them to know it; and to know that God loved them too, and wanted them to love him and be happy."

Elfie had never had any one to love her in all her life, and she could but dimly understand what Susie meant; but she did understand it a little, and all the vain longings she had felt when looking at a mother kissing her child sprung up in her heart now, as she said, in a subdued, gentle voice, "I wish he'd love me just a little."

"He does love you," said Susie, "not a little, but a great deal."

"Did he tell you to tell me so?" asked Elfie eagerly.

Susie knew not what to reply to this; but the thought stole into her heart—Was this the work her mother had spoken of—was she to tell Elfie of the love of God, try to make her understand it, and lead her to love him?

But her silence made Elfie think she had no message for her, and she said, "You need not be afraid to tell me, Susie; nobody ever did love me, and nobody ever will; and I don't want any love either." But in spite of these words, so sharply and angrily spoken, Elfie burst into tears.

Susie had never seen her cry before, and for very sympathy she burst into tears herself, as she threw her arms round her companion's neck, and drew her closely towards her. "Don't cry, Elfie; I'll love you," she said. "I'll love you ever so much; and you'll believe God loves you too; won't you?" she added coaxingly.

Elfie clung to Susie, and held her in a passionate embrace. "Say it again—" she whispered, "say you love me, Susie; it's what I've been wanting ever so long, I think."

"Everybody wants it," said Susie. "God puts the feeling in our heart, mother said; and then he gives us people to love us, just that we may know how he loves us himself."

"Tell me some more about it," said Elfie, still in the same subdued voice, and clinging fast round Susie's neck, her dirty tangled head of hair resting on her shoulder.

"I don't know how to tell it, Elfie, but just as the Bible tells it. Mother made me learn a good many verses about the love of God. I'll tell you some of them. 'God is love'; 'Like as a father pitieth his children, so the Lord pitieth them that fear him'; 'God so loved the world, that he gave his only begotten Son, that whosoever believeth in him should not perish, but have everlasting life.' Now, don't you see God must love you, for you're in the world, and God so loved the world that he sent Jesus Christ to die that we might be saved?"

"Saved?" repeated Elfie.

"Yes; saved from our sins—the wicked things we do that make God sorry, and angry too," said Susie.

But Elfie did not care to hear about this; she wanted to know whether it was possible for God to love her—whether he had told Susie, he would love her.

"I'd do anything for that," she said, pushing back her tangled hair. "Do you think he'd like me better if I was to keep my face clean and comb my hair like you do?" she asked.

Susie smiled. "I think God does like people to be clean," she said; "and I'd like it, Elfie."

"Then I'll do it," said Elfie in a determined tone. "I've thought it was no good. Before, I was just street rubbish, and nobody cared for me; but if you do, and God will, I'll wash my face; and perhaps he will by-and-by, as the Lord Jesus his Son was a poor man himself."

And Elfie went at once to fetch some water to wash her face, and Susie promised to help her to do her hair.

CHAPTER III
OUR FATHER

FROM this time Elfie began to pay some attention to her personal appearance. She washed her face and hands, and combed her hair every morning, before she went out, and, of course, looked less wild; but her rags, poor child, were past mending, and there seemed no hope of ever being able to replace these with better clothes now. New ones—new frocks, new shoes, that gave other little girls so much pleasure—Elfie had never had. Sometimes she wore a pair of old shoes or boots picked up in the street, and sometimes she went barefoot. And it was much the same with frocks and bonnets: sometimes she picked up a rag that would cover her, or had one given her, and she wore it until it dropped to pieces. She had never been quite naked; but many times she had been almost so, until some one had given her something to put on.

She began to wish now that some one would do so again; and formed all sorts of plans for saving enough money to buy herself a frock at a second-hand clothes' stall—plans that always failed, for winter was drawing near, and the two girls found it harder work than ever to pay the rent and buy bread to eat.

"The rent must be paid," Elfie said over and over again, as if to convince herself of a fact she half doubted.

Susie said nothing, but stitched away as fast as she could, and always contrived to have the shilling for the landlord when he called; for she knew if it were not paid, they would be turned into the street, and for Elfie's sake, as well as her own, she did not wish this to happen. Elfie said she did not care, she had always been used to a street life, but that it would never do for Susie; and so for her sake—to keep Susie's home for her—she grew more careful and steady, that she might be trusted by people to do odd jobs for them, and thus bring in a few pence to add to the weekly store.

But with all Elfie's care and steadiness, and Susie's close stitching, they had a hard time of it to make ends meet; and Susie grew pale and weak, and often suffered from pain in her side. She went regularly to church on Sunday, but she could never persuade Elfie to do so. Church was for decent folk, not for her, she said; but she looked forward to sitting down with her arms round Susie's neck, to listen to her reading from the Bible, on Sunday afternoon.

Sometimes they contrived to have a fire on Sunday, but it was not often they could have one all the week, except to boil the kettle occasionally; for Susie still kept up the habit of having regular meals, and was gradually winning Elfie to like this plan too.

People began to notice the pale, pinched little face under the shabby black bonnet, that was seen so regularly every Sunday in a quiet corner of the church; and at length, a lady spoke to her as she was coming out one day.

"Where do you live, little girl?" asked the lady kindly.

It was very cold, and the lady could not help shivering in her warm furs, and she noticed that Susie had only a thin cape on.

"In Fisher's Lane, please, ma'am," answered Susie, dropping a courtesy and blushing.

But the lady did not know Fisher's Lane. "Do you go to the Ragged School?" she asked.

Susie shook her head. "I don't know where it is," she said.

"That is a pity," said the lady, "for there is a Sunday school there afternoon and evening, in a nice, warm room, and the teachers would be glad to see you, I am sure."

"Would they?" said Susie. "I used to go to Sunday school before we came to live here. Perhaps Elfie knows where it is, and maybe she'll come with me."

"Ask her," said the lady; "we shall be very glad to see you both."

She did not stay to ask who Elfie was; but she looked after Susie as she ran down the street, and was surprised to see her join poor, ragged, neglected-looking Elfie—for Susie still contrived to keep a decent appearance, although her clothes were so thin and old.

The lady's invitation was repeated to Elfie; but to Susie's surprise she did not look at all pleased.

"Do you know where the school is?" asked Susie.

Elfie nodded. "Yes, I know where it is, but I shan't go."

"O Elfie, do," said Susie coaxingly.

"No, I shan't. You may, if you want to leave me all alone on Sunday afternoons," said Elfie sulkily.

"But I don't want to leave you, Elfie; want you to come with me," said Susie.

"I don't want to come," said Elfie doggedly.

"Why not?" persistently asked Susie.

"I don't like schools, nor them that go to 'em." And to end all further discussion on the subject, Elfie ran home, leaving Susie to follow more leisurely.

There was nothing for her to hurry home for. The room looked cold, bare, and desolate, for they could not indulge in a fire to-day; they had not been able to make up the rent money, and the thought of this had troubled Susie until she went to church. There, however, she had heard the message bidding her to cast her care upon God; and she came home to the cheerless room, and her dinner of dry bread, feeling as blithe as a bird.

"Why, what's come to you, Susie?" asked Elfie. "You was crying and fretting about the rent money before you went out, and now you look as though you'd got it all safe in the tin box."

The mention of the rent brought a little cloud into Susie's face, but it was quickly dispelled as she answered, "O Elfie, I wish you could have heard the minister to-day, and what he said about God taking care of us."

"It don't seem as though he took much care of you and me," said Elfie sulkily, as she looked at the empty grate, and tried to draw her rags over her bare shoulders.

"Are you very cold, Elfie?" asked Susie tenderly.

"I shouldn't think you was very warm," said Elfie crossly. "Your frock ain't in rags perhaps, but it's as thin as mine."

"Yes, it is thin," said Susie, "and I'm cold; but it seems to me God does care even for our being cold, for he's sent to tell us we may go where there is a fire this afternoon."

"Where's that?" asked Elfie sharply.

"At the school the lady told me about," answered Susie. "She said there was a fire there, and that they would be very glad to see us."

"Well, I shan't go," said Elfie. "I'd rather stop here in the cold."

This seemed unreasonable to Susie. "Do tell me why you won't go?" she said.

"No, I shan't. And if you go, don't you tell anybody you know me," said Elfie.

"Why not? Have you been to the school before?" asked Susie.

"I shan't tell you, and I won't go," said Elfie doggedly.

Susie was puzzled. She hardly knew what to do, for she did not like to leave Elfie, and yet she wanted to go to school. But at length she decided to stay at home and read to her companion, and go to the school in the evening, if Elfie would show her the way; for they had no fire and no candle to burn to-night, and it would be very dull to sit there in the dark listening to the noises in the other lodgers' rooms, for there was rarely a Sunday evening passed without a quarrel in the house. Elfie would go out to play with some of her companions as soon as it grew dusk; but Susie had given up going out to play on Sunday.

After a little persuasion, Elfie agreed to take Susie to the corner of the street where the school was; but she would not go any further, and she promised to meet her at the same corner when she came out after school.

"But I don't know what time the school will be over," said Susie.

"I do," said Elfie with a short laugh; "but mind you ain't to tell any of 'em who showed you the way," she added in a more serious tone.

Susie promised not to mention her name, and she hoped the lady who had invited her would forget that she had said she would bring Elfie with her; but she could not help thinking it very strange that Elfie should dislike the idea of coming so much.

The children had begun to assemble when she reached the school; and hardly knowing where she was going, Susie went into the large, light, warm room, and looked round for the lady whom she had seen in the morning. She was not there, but another teacher came forward and asked her name, and where she lived; and on hearing she could read put her into the Bible class at once.

Susie looked shyly at her companions, who were, of course, looking at her, but not very shyly, for many of them looked as though they were used to a street life, and most of them were older than herself. What a treat it was to these poor girls to sit down in a warm, light room, Susie could only guess. To her it was very delightful—the mere sensation of light and warmth; and the only drawback to her enjoyment was the thought that poor Elfie was not sharing it.

She could join in singing the opening hymn; and then, when the books were given out, she found her place more quickly than the rest, and ventured to lift her eyes to the teacher's face for a minute, and then saw that the lady was looking at her.

"You have not been to the school before, have you, my dear?" she said in a gentle voice.

"No, ma'am," answered Susie.

"I hope we shall see you very often now. Can you come every Sunday?" said the lady.

"Yes, ma'am," replied Susie.

And then, the others having found their places, the reading commenced. The lady explained the meaning of each verse as they went on, but spoke more particularly of God's care for his children.

When school was over, and Susie met Elfie, she told her of the evening lesson, and how like it was to what she had heard in the morning; but Elfie answered, "I'm going to take care of myself now, and then perhaps God will do it for me by-and-by."

"I think we need God's care now," sighed Susie, thinking of the deficient store of halfpence in the tin box at home.

"Well, we don't get it," said Elfie defiantly; "and going to that school won't bring it neither. Don't go again, Susie," she added.

"But I like it; and I must go now, because I've promised," said Susie. "I do wish you would go with me, it is so nice, Elfie. We sing, and read, and pray to God; and the room is so beautiful with the fire and the gas."

"I know all about it," said Elfie sulkily; "and I know just what you'll do too: you'll go to that school, and then you won't like me. Some of 'em 'll tell you I'm a bad girl, and then you won't speak to me." And the thought of this so overcame poor Elfie that she burst into tears.

Susie put her arm round her neck, and drew her own thin cape over her shoulders. "Nobody shall make me say that about you, Elfie," she said. "Don't cry. I'll love you always; and you shall come to school with me, and learn to read."

But Elfie still shook her head about going to school. "I can't go there," she said.

"Yes, you shall, Elfie. I know why you don't like to go; it's because your frock is so old. But we'll try and make another this week. I think mother would like you to have her frock to go to school in," she added. "And there's her shawl; perhaps we could make two of it; and I don't think she'd mind, as we are so cold."

Susie was determined that nothing should damp her happiness to-night, and she would not listen to Elfie's refusal to go to school. She felt brave, too, or she could not have spoken about cutting up her mother's dress and wearing her shawl as she did. Yes, the little girl was brave and hopeful. What she had heard of God's care and tender love to-day had brought back all the lessons of her childhood; and she could believe that God was her Father, and cared—really cared for and loved her.

When they reached home she said, "I wish you'd kneel down and say 'Our Father' of a night, like I do, Elfie."

"But I don't know it," said Elfie.

"Well, I'll teach you, shall I? You can say it after me in bed until you know it by yourself; only, I'd like you to kneel down and say it first, like I did to mother."

Elfie was generally willing to do anything to please her companion, and she very readily consented to this. And so, after shutting the door, the two girls knelt down in the pale moonlight beside a chair, and Elfie repeated the words slowly and reverently as Susie uttered them—the divine words that make all men brothers and all women sisters.

There must have been some such thought as this in Susie's mind, for as she crept into bed after Elfie she said, "I did not think of it before, but you are my sister, Elfie, so I shall never forget to love you;" and she kissed her as she spoke.

Elfie threw her arms round her. "Say you'll love me always," she whispered; "for there's nobody else in all the world if you don't."

"I do love you," said Susie. "But oh, Elfie, I wish you'd believe God loves you too—that he is our Father."

"I don't know nothing about fathers; I never had a father," said Elfie. "But if you'll love me, perhaps I shall believe that God does, by-and-by—especially as the Lord Jesus was a poor man. I like to hear about that, because, you see, it makes it seem somehow that he knows all about poor people—even street rubbish like I am, if he had no bed and no home."

Before they went to sleep that night, Elfie had learned to repeat the Lord's Prayer almost perfectly (she could learn quickly if she liked); and at last dropped to sleep murmuring the words, "Our Father—our Father." And Susie thought over all she had heard that day of the heavenly Father's love; and at last fell asleep, to dream that her mother had come back to lift all the care off her shoulders, and shelter her from every rough wind that blew.

But Monday morning brought the every-day anxiety with it; and Susie's first thought was of the landlord, and what he would say when he came in the afternoon and found she had only tenpence of the rent saved up in the tin box. She tried to recall something of what she had heard the previous day—tried to cast her care upon God; but it was very hard; and it was not until she had knelt down and prayed, ay, and sobbed out her trouble before him, that she could believe any of it this morning, although she had felt so sure of it the day before.

Elfie had woke up first and gone out. She often did this if there was only a small piece of bread in the house, because then she could leave the bread for Susie, and pick up her breakfast at the market, or about the streets.

So, after eating her bread, Susie took out her work, sitting upon the low stool, with the blanket of the bed wrapped round her, for it was bitterly cold this morning, and they had no fire. They had been afraid to buy coals or wood, as they could not make up the rent. This was Susie's great anxiety this morning. What the landlord would say, she did not know. He was a gruff, cross man; and Susie dreaded his visit—sat trembling with fear at the thought of hearing him come up the stairs; and again and again lifted her heart in asking that they might not be turned out of their home.

CHAPTER IV
ELFIE'S SIXPENCE

SUSIE'S suspense as to the result of the landlord's visit came to an end sooner than she expected. He called earlier than usual to-day, and the poor girl's last faint hope that Elfie would be able to earn twopence and get back before he came was cut off as she heard his halting footsteps coming up the stairs. He knocked at the opposite door first, and Susie hoped he would be detained there, and she crept to the top of the stairs and looked over, in the hope of seeing Elfie coming up.

But Elfie was not to be seen; and with a sinking heart, Susie went back and took down the tin box, and then sat down to her work again, waiting for the door to open and Elfie to come in, for somehow she had persuaded herself that she would come in yet. But in a minute or two, the opposite door closed, and then there was a knock at her own. Susie could hardly walk across the room to open it, she trembled so violently.

"Good morning," said the landlord pleasantly, as he stepped in and looked round the room. "You keep the place nice and clean," he said approvingly. "But why don't you have a fire, child? It's cold to-day, and you sitting at your sewing."

"Yes, sir," said Susie meekly, glancing at the empty grate, and hardly knowing how to tell him she had not been able to make up the rent.

"You ought to have a fire," went on the man, not noticing her confusion, and wishing to say something kind to the poor little orphan. "You ought to have a fire this cold day; every other room in the house has one."

"Have they, sir?" said Susie, thinking the man was displeased. "I'm very sorry I can't get one too; but I don't think the place will get damp—we have one sometimes."

"The place get damp!" repeated the landlord. "What do you mean, child?"

"Please, sir, I thought you was afraid the room would spoil," said Susie, still dreading to make the revelation that she had only tenpence of the rent.

"Spoil!" repeated the man. And he looked round on the patched, discoloured walls, and laughed. "Why, child, you keep your room nicer than any other in the house. I was thinking you must be cold."

"I don't mind that much, sir, if I can only stay here," said Susie; "but—but please, sir, I've only got tenpence of the rent to-day. I hope you won't turn us out for the other twopence. I'll try and pay it next week, sir," she added.

The man took the halfpence and counted them, and then looked at the little pale, pinched face before him. He loved money, and was used to scenes of misery, but was not quite without human feeling, and Susie's mute distress was almost more than he could look upon unmoved. "Who told you I should turn you out, child?" he said.

"No one, but—but I was afraid you would if I didn't keep the rent paid," said Susie.

"Yes, to be sure—of course I should—I can't do without my rent," said the landlord; "but still, in the case of a little girl that's honest and tries to do her best, I shouldn't be hard on her for twopence. But you mustn't let the others know I said this," he added quickly.

"No, sir; and I'll try to pay it next week," answered Susie with a sigh of relief; as the man turned towards the door.

"Good-bye, child," said the man, still toying with the halfpence he held in his hand. Susie thought he had gone, and took up her work again, but the next minute he was back.

"Never mind about the twopence next week," he said in a hurried whisper: "and look here, child; I don't like to think of you sitting here without a fire: go and buy some wood and coals with this." And as he spoke he laid fourpence on the table, and then hurried to the door again.

Susie could not thank him, she could only look her dumb surprise, and then burst into tears. While he stumped downstairs, wondering what could have made him give back to the girl half a week's rent.

Susie knew how it was, although her landlord did not, and still sobbing, she knelt down to thank God for his loving care of her. As soon as her tears had subsided a little, and she could smile at the thought of her anticipated trouble that never came, she got up and went out to buy some wood and coals to light a fire; for she ought to do this, she thought, as the money had been given her for that purpose. She wanted to surprise Elfie, too, by getting up a bright blaze before she came in; so that she was rather disappointed, when she returned with her load, to see Elfie sitting down by the empty grate.

The coals were heavy, although there was only a small quantity, and Susie was panting for breath as she pushed open the door; but Elfie did not lift her head from her knees, where she had buried her face, as she sat crouching on the floor.

"What's the matter?" asked Susie in some alarm, as she lifted the coals on to the hearth.

"Nothing," replied Elfie, without raising her head.

Susie thought she knew what it was. "Look up, Elfie," she said, in a tone of gladness: "the landlord's been here, and it's all right now; and see what I've got."

Elfie slowly raised her head, but did not look at Susie or the bag of coals. "The landlord's been here," she slowly repeated; "then I'm too late after all;" and her head went down lower than before.

Susie was puzzled, until looking round she saw a little pile of halfpence on the table. "O Elfie, where did you get all that money?" she said in a tone of joyful surprise, as she sprang over to count it. "Sixpence! O Elfie, how rich we are! And I've just been to buy some coals to make a fire. But why don't you look up?" she added, as she noticed that her companion's head was still bowed upon her knees.

But Elfie did not move, did not attempt to lift her head, but grumbled out something Susie could not understand.

"Are you ill, Elfie?" asked Susie in alarm.

"No, no; leave me alone, and light the fire," said the girl, shaking off the hand that had been laid upon her shoulder.

"I know what it is: you're sorry you did not get home in time to pay the landlord. But it doesn't matter one bit; he was very kind, and won't turn us out, and we ain't to pay the twopence next week. Wouldn't you like to know how I got the coals?" said Susie.

"How did you get 'em?" said Elfie, just lifting her head for a minute.

"Hold your head up, then, and tell me how you got all that money on the table first," said Susie laughing.

But Elfie's head went down again at once. "I don't want to know about the coals," she said; "you can keep your secret and I'll keep mine."

"But it isn't a secret, Elfie. I'll tell you all about it," said Susie, beginning to place the wood in the grate, for she could not afford to waste her time.

"I don't want to know," replied Elfie. "Perhaps the angels your mother talked about brought you the money," she added.

"Did the angels bring yours?" asked Susie.

For answer, Elfie started from her seat, gave Susie a violent blow on her back, and rushed downstairs and out into the street.

As soon as Susie could recover from the blow, she ran out of the room calling, "Elfie! Elfie!" But Elfie was half-way up the lane by that time, and did not hear the call; and if she had, she would probably have run away the faster. When Susie went back she looked at the money that still lay on the table, wondering what could have made Elfie so cross. She could not understand this sudden change in her behaviour at all; she had always been so kind to her before, and it seemed hard to believe that it was Elfie who had struck her now.

After watching the fire for a minute or two, she washed her hands and sat down to work again, feeling very sad and uncomfortable, and wondering when Elfie would come back. Then she wondered whether she had had anything to eat to-day; she herself was hungry, and yet she had eaten a slice of bread, and had not been running about the streets as Elfie had.

"Oh, that has made her cross. She was so hungry, and yet she would not spend any money till she had brought it home, and then it was too late for the landlord. Poor Elfie! But never mind, we'll have a nice, real tea to-day." And as she spoke, Susie put on the tea-kettle, and then went out to buy the things for the real tea.

Just as it was getting dusk she got the tea ready, and then sat down to wait for Elfie's coming. But an hour passed and no one came; and then, feeling faint and almost sick with hunger, she took her tea by herself, feeling sadly disappointed that Elfie had not come home.

Elfie did not make her appearance until bed-time, and then she crept in, looking as cross and sullen as when she went out. Susie had forgotten her unkindness of the afternoon, and jumped up at once to meet her.

"O Elfie, why didn't you come before?" she said. "I got such a nice tea ready for you. But never mind; I've kept the teapot on the hob, so it's hot now, I daresay;" and she went to pour it out.

"I don't want any tea," said Elfie. "Where's the money I left on the table?"

"Did you want it? O Elfie, I've spent it," said Susie in dismay.

"Oh, it don't matter," said Elfie carelessly, beginning to take off some of her clothes, ready to go to bed.

"Won't you have some tea? Oh, do, Elfie," said Susie. "I'm sure you must be hungry. See, I've cut some bread for you, all ready."

But Elfie shook her head. "I don't want it," she said; "I'm not hungry." And in spite of all Susie's coaxing, she went to bed without touching a bit.

Susie had a great mind to cry. She felt so vexed; and she thought Elfie was cross now because she had spent the sixpence. She could not work any longer; so, putting out the candle, she undressed and crept into bed beside Elfie, who pretended to be fast asleep.

Susie found out, at last, that she was awake, and creeping closer to her she said, "I'm so sorry I spent the sixpence, Elfie; it seems so greedy of me."

"Bother the sixpence! Don't talk about that any more," said Elfie crossly.

"What shall we talk about?" said Susie. "I'm not at all sleepy, and I wanted to talk to you, to tell you how good 'our Father' had been to us to-day," she added in a whisper.

Elfie flounced herself over, pulling all the bed-clothes off Susie. "You're always talking about that," she said crossly.

Susie did not know what to say, and she felt so hurt that she burst into tears.

For a few minutes Elfie lay quite still; but at length she turned round and put the clothes over Susie's shoulders, saying, "There, don't cry, Susie. I'm such a wretch. I'll go away to-morrow."

But Susie's tears only fell the faster. "O Elfie, what have I done? I'm so sorry I spent the sixpence; but don't go away to-morrow, and I'll work and get you another." And she threw her arms round her companion's neck, and kissed her.

Elfie was crying too now. "I'd better go away, Susie," she said. "I'm a bad, wicked girl, and you'd better not love me any more."

"But I do love you," sobbed Susie. "O Elfie, don't go away and leave me!"

"But you can't love me now, Susie! I hit you this afternoon," said Elfie through her tears.

"I made you cross first. O Elfie, I did not think you wanted that sixpence for anything, and it was greedy of me to spend it!"

"No, it wasn't," said Elfie; "but don't talk about that any more. I want to forget all about it."

"Why?" asked Susie. "I like to think how I get my money, 'specially when somebody's kind, like the landlord was to-day. Don't you think it was God put it into his heart to give me fourpence, and not be cross about the rent?"

"I suppose it was," assented Elfie; "but I don't want to think about God any more, so don't talk about him."

"Don't want to think about God!" repeated Susie. "O Elfie, and you'd begun to say 'our Father,' and liked to hear me talk about the Lord Jesus being a poor man."

"Well, I don't want to hear any more about him; and I shan't say 'our Father' any more. He ain't my Father now," said Elfie doggedly.

"Why not? O Elfie! And he's been so good to us to-day," said Susie.

"Yes, I suppose he is good; and he makes me feel bad, and I never did feel so till to-day, so I'm going to forget him."

"O Elfie! And make him feel so sad and sorry about you," said Susie.

"Now, don't talk like that, or else I shall cry," said Elfie with a stifled sob. "I don't want you to love me now."

"But I can't help loving you—I will love you," said Susie passionately.

And instead of pushing her away, Elfie returned her caresses, and the two girls cried for some time, without speaking a word to each other.

At length Elfie said, "It makes me glad and sorry too, Susie."

"What does?" asked Susie.

"That you love me so. I didn't think you would after I hit you this afternoon. I'm so sorry I did it."

"Oh, never mind; I know you didn't mean to hurt me," said Susie cheerfully. "I know you loved me all the time."

"Yes, I do love you, Susie; but somehow I wish you didn't love me now," said Elfie with a deep sigh.

"Why?" asked Susie, in a tone of surprise.

"Because it ain't no good loving me; I'm bad. I didn't know I was till to-day; but I am, and you'd better not love me any more. God don't, I know," said Elfie.

"Yes, he does," said Susie quickly. "He loves you, Elfie, more than I can. He is—"

"There, hold your tongue. I don't want to hear about him," interrupted Elfie.

Susie was puzzled, but remained silent for a minute or two, and then asked—"Where have you been to-day, Elfie?"

"Oh, lots of places," she answered shortly. "But don't ask about that; tell me what you've been doing."

"Working, to be sure," answered Susie. There was nothing to tell beyond this. Her life was summed up in these words, for there was no change in it, save the weekly walk to take her work home.

Elfie's, on the contrary, was full of change, amid all its sameness in wandering; for there was constantly something happening, either in the streets or the market; and wherever a crowd collected, Elfie was sure to be; and from the remarks of the bystanders, she learned all that had happened, and was delighted to tell Susie when she returned home, so that her unwillingness to speak of this now was the more remarkable.

There seemed nothing they could talk about after Susie had given an account of the landlord's visit, and so they soon dropped asleep—Susie hoping that Ellie would tell her all about the sixpence the next day, and Elfie wishing Susie would soon forget all about it.

A fresh disappointment as the next morning. She had resolved to get up early, and prepare a "real breakfast," that Elfie might have some before she went out. But Elfie woke first, and went off without waking her, or taking any of the bread that had been cut the night before; and, contrary to her usual practice, she stayed out the whole of the day.

CHAPTER V
SAVED BY LOVE

SUSIE could not understand the alteration in Elfie, but altered she certainly was. Sometimes she would stay away for two or three days together, and then come home and be as affectionate as ever, and give Susie all the money she had been able to get; but she would never tell her how she got it or where she had been. Then, after staying about in the same neighbourhood, she would go off no one knew where, leaving Susie to lie listening for her to come home at night, and to feel very dull and lonely by herself.

Poor Susie had other anxieties to trouble her, too, besides those she suffered on Elfie's account. Work was becoming scarce; and soon after the winter set in, she was told she had better look out for something else to do, as they could not give her the sewing much longer.

"What shall I do—what can I do?" said Susie, when she told Elfie of this.

"I must get some more money," said Elfie. "I daresay I can get enough for both of us, and then you need not do this work."

"But can't I help you?" asked Susie. "I shouldn't like you to do everything."

"You can't help me get money," said Elfie evasively.

"Oh, I won't mind going into the market with you, if you'll ask the men to let me mind the baskets as well as you," said Susie.

Elfie laughed. "You couldn't," she said.

"Oh yes, I could—I would," added Susie. "I'd do anything to earn some money."

"Could you fight the boys if they came to take the things?" asked Elfie.

Susie shook her head, and looked greatly disappointed. "Oh, what can I do?" she said. "This is the last lot of shirts I shall have to make, and I must do something to earn some money."

Elfie thought for a minute or two of all the means she had tried to earn money, but there was only one in which Susie was likely to succeed.

"You might clean doorsteps," she said slowly.

"Oh yes; mother taught me how to clean the hearth and scrub the floor," said Susie quickly.

"Can you clean knives and forks as well?" asked Elfie.

Susie nodded. "I know how to do all sorts of cleaning," she said.

"I don't," said Elfie; "I can just clean steps. And so when the people asked me to clean the knives and forks, and I couldn't, they wouldn't let me do the steps. But if you can do all sorts of work, you can soon get some. I'll show you how to manage."

Elfie kept her word. As soon as the last bundle of shirts was carried home, and before the money was expended, the two girls went out together in search of some employment for Susie.

A short distance from Fisher's Lane there was a respectable neighbourhood, where the people seemed to pride themselves on the neatness of their doorsteps, but where very few could afford to keep servants to clean them. Here Elfie had often earned a few pence, and might have gained more, if she could have done more than clean the steps. For occasionally she had been asked to clean knives and forks, and windows. There she brought Susie, and boldly knocked at a door, asking if they wanted the steps cleaned.

"Not to-day," answered the woman; "and besides, the girl who cleans my steps must do the knives and forks as well."

"She can clean knives and all sorts of things," said Elfie, pushing Susie forward.

The woman looked at her. "Have you learned to scrub?" she asked.

"Yes, ma'am," answered Susie quietly.

"Well, then, you may come to me to-morrow and I'll give you something to do."

Susie was delighted, and Elfie looked pleased. "You'll be sure to get on now," she said complacently.

"Do you clean all these steps?" asked Susie, looking down the neat quiet street.

Elfie laughed. "I don't clean steps now, I tell you," she said, rather sharply.

"Why not?" asked Susie; "Do you get so many baskets to mind now?" she asked.

"I don't mind baskets either," said Elfie fiercely. "I'm just street rubbish—just what people said I was long ago; and I don't care a bit. No, I don't care; and I won't care," she added, "though you do talk about that school, and try to coax me to go with you."

Susie looked at her angry face in silent surprise. What could have provoked this outbreak she could not tell, for she had not ventured to mention the Ragged School to her for some weeks past, although she had not given up all hope of persuading her to go with her.

"Elfie, what's the matter—what do you mean?" she asked.

Elfie looked somewhat subdued. "Why, you're not to bother me about what I do to get the money," she said, rather more quietly. "I cleaned steps as long as I could, but I never had anybody to teach me to do things like you had; and then the people in the market called me a thief, and I couldn't get the baskets to mind."

"Never mind, Elfie; I know you ain't a thief, and I love you," said Susie, in a gentle, soothing voice.

But Elfie shrunk away from the proffered caress. "I'm bad, I tell you, and don't want you to love me."

"Oh, but I will love you, even if you are bad," said Susie with a smile.

The altercation ended, as usual, in both girls promising they would never leave each other; but a feeling of uneasiness was left in Susie's mind, and she could not get rid of the wish to know more about the way in which Elfie spent her time now. She loved her companion very dearly, in spite of her strange behaviour sometimes, and she wished Elfie would tell her how she got the money she brought home. It was often silver now, as well as pence; but the possession of it never seemed to give her any pleasure, and she was sure to be fierce and angry if she asked where it came from, and would refuse to eat anything that was bought with it!

This was very puzzling to Susie, and the more she thought about it, the more unhappy did she become. And yet she was afraid to tell Elfie of her unhappiness, for fear she should put her oft repeated threat into execution, and never come home any more.

She was earning a little money still herself, but she could not depend upon earning a regular amount as when she did the sewing; for people did not want their steps cleaned every day. She managed to give satisfaction in this new work, and the first to employ her, recommended her to several neighbours; but it was only one or two days a week that she was wanted, and the rest of her time passed very slowly if Elfie did not come home all day.

One morning Susie thought she would walk a little further, and venture to inquire in another direction if a girl was wanted to do house work. She had heard that girls sometimes could get a place to go to every morning, and have part of their meals each day. Now, if she could do this it would be so much pleasanter, and she would not mind how hard she had to work; and she made up her mind to inquire for such a place as this before she left home.

Which way to turn she did not know, and she stood at the top of Fisher's Lane looking up and down the road debating this point, until at length she lifted her heart in silent prayer to God to guide her aright. Then she walked cheerfully on down the road for some distance, until she came to some quiet side streets, and at the corner of one of these, she went into a grocer shop, and asked if they knew any one who wanted a girl.

The man asked her how old she was, and what work she could do; and then told her his wife wanted some one to help her with the work in the morning, and asked her to step into the back parlour and speak to her. Susie's heart beat high with hope as she went into the room, while the grocer called his wife. Surely God had directed her steps, that she should hear of what she wanted so soon!

The grocer's wife asked Susie a good many questions, but seemed to be satisfied with her answers. She could not, however, quite decide about taking her, she said; she must talk to her husband first: she did not know what he would say about taking her without a character, and from such a bad place as Fisher's Lane, too, and so she must come again the next morning.

Susie promised to do so, hoping the answer would be favourable, for she thought she should be very comfortable working under such a kind mistress; and then the wages offered—eighteen-pence a week and her breakfast and dinner—seemed to promise almost riches. Her heart was light although it trembled with anxious expectation as she went through the shop again.

Just as she reached the street she noticed there was a little commotion lower down—a group of boys and girls, and a policeman half dragging, half carrying somebody along. Susie's heart almost stood still as she caught sight of the little ragged culprit, and she could only totter forward a few steps past the grocer, who had stepped out on to the pavement, when she became sure it was Elfie in the policeman's hands! "O Elfie, Elfie I what is it; what is the matter?" said Susie, darting forward.

At the sound of her voice Elfie ceased her struggles. "Go away, Susie," she muttered hoarsely, staring at her wildly.

"No, no, I can't go away," said Susie, trying to catch hold of her frock. "Tell me what it is, Elfie."

"No need to ask what it is," laughed two or three boys: "she's a regular little thief, she is; but she's caught at last, and serve her right."

Elfie looked defiant, and renewed her kicking and struggling; but Susie burst into tears. "Oh, don't take her away," she sobbed, appealing to the policeman; "oh, please let her come home with me, and she'll never do it any more."

"Home with you!" said the man roughly. "Then you're one of the Fisher Lane thieves too, I suppose?"

Susie's pale face flushed and a look of shame stole over it; but still she did not attempt to leave Elfie's side, although she knew all that crowd of boys and girls were staring at her and calling her a thief as well as Elfie.

"Why don't you go away, Susie? I don't want you; I never want to see you any more," said Elfie, in a hard, defiant tone.

But Susie did not go away. They had got into the broad open road now, and everybody turned to look at them—looks that seemed to crush poor Susie and make her heart almost stand still with horror and anguish; but still she kept on walking in the centre of the little crowd.

"If Elfie has been stealing, you must take me up too," she said to the policeman, "for I had part of the money."

"I daresay you did. There's a nice lot of thieves round in Fisher's Lane, I know," said the man.

And as the gates of the police station were reached, he took good care that they should close on Susie too.

She had no wish to escape, although she trembled as they entered a room where another man asked their names and where they lived.

While this was being done, the policeman who had brought them, whispered to one of the others, and then they were taken to a dark room and locked up. Elfie screamed with terror as the door closed, and they were left standing there in the cold, dark room, with only the rift of daylight that struggled through the grating high up in the wall. Susie shuddered, but she was not so frightened as Elfie, who fell sobbing on her neck.

Susie clasped her arms round her. "What is it, Elfie? What have you done?" asked Susie in a whisper.

"Just what they said. I've done it many a time," sobbed Elfie; "but I didn't do it to-day, for I saw somebody coming, and put the boots down."

"O Elfie! You've been stealing," said Susie sadly.

Elfie tried to twist herself away from Susie. "Why don't you say you hate me? I know you do," she said.

"No, I don't, Elfie, or else I shouldn't have come to prison with you," said Susie, holding her more tightly in her arms.

Elfie yielded to the loving embrace and sobbed again. "That's the worst of it," she said. "I shouldn't care so much for what the policemen could do to me, if you didn't know about it."

"But God would know, if I did not," said Susie, in a gentle whisper.

Elfie shuddered. "Does God know everything?" she said.

"Yes; everything we say and do," answered Susie. "He knows how many times you stole things, although you may forget."

"Well, I don't care," said Elfie defiantly. "He don't love me."

"O Elfie, he does; and it makes him sorry, and angry too, when we do anything that is wrong;" and Susie burst into tears.

"Don't cry, don't cry, Susie, and I'll never do it any more. I'll try and get some honest work, though it is so hard," said Elfie, and her tears broke out afresh. The two sat down together on the hard, cold floor, and with their arms round each other's necks, Elfie promised never to steal again, if Susie would leave off crying and love her still. "I will try to be honest, and mind the baskets, and clean steps," she sobbed. "But they called me a thief when I wasn't; and then when we wanted that twopence for the rent, and I couldn't get it any other way, I thought I'd steal it, only you shouldn't know."

"O Elfie, did you steal that sixpence?" asked Susie.

Elfie sobbed. "I stole some things and sold 'em to get that," she said; "that was the first time since I'd known you," she added.

"Did you steal before?" asked Susie.

"Yes, sometimes, when I was very hungry. And they knew it at the Ragged School; that was why I wouldn't go with you," said Elfie, who seemed determined to make a full confession now.

"What did you steal?" asked Susie.

"All sorts of things—anything I could see in shops and run away with. I never felt bad about it before; but when I took the things to get that sixpence for the rent, I felt I was wicked, and God seemed to be looking at me all the time, though I wanted to forget all about him."

"Yes, God was looking at you," said Susie; "and he was sorry about you too—more sorry than I can be, because he loves you more than I do."

"More than you do!" repeated Elfie. "He can't, for you've come to prison with me, though all the people were looking at you and calling you a thief."

"Yes, he has," said Susie. "Don't you remember I told you about the Lord Jesus being God as well as man? Well, he came down from heaven to die for our sins—to save us just because we had all been doing such wicked things as stealing, and telling lies, and forgetting him. But to do this he had to suffer a dreadful, cruel death. And he wasn't compelled to do it either, for he did not deserve it; it was us who deserved it, but he loved us so much that he took our punishment instead."

"But he won't love me now," said Elfie. "It's no good telling me about this now."

"Yes, it is. Elfie, if you will only ask him to help you to be honest in future," said Susie.

"But I've been stealing—I've done such lots of bad things," said Elfie.

"But Jesus will forgive them all, if you ask him," said Susie quickly. "He loves you still, Elfie; though you've been trying to forget him, he hasn't forgot you. He wants you to believe in his love and love him too."

"O Susie, are you sure about it? Are you sure Jesus will love me as much as you do?" asked Elfie.

"He loves you a great deal more than I do. That's why God wishes us to love each other, that we may understand his love," said Susie. "Mother used to say we could never understand God's love, if it wasn't for having father and mother or brothers and sisters to love us."

"I never had a father and mother to love me," said Elfie. "I never had anybody but you, Susie."

"Never mind; I'll be your sister, and love you," said Susie.

"And then, perhaps, by-and-by I shall understand about God's love," whispered Elfie, as she laid her head Susie's shoulder.

CHAPTER VI
WILL SHE CONQUER?

AFTER Elfie and Susie had been kept some hours in the dull, gloomy prison cell, a policeman came and took them into another part of the building, where a magistrate was sitting, and the policeman stated why Elfie had been taken up. He had not seen her take the boots himself, however, and the man to whom they belonged said he did not wish to send the child to prison; and so the magistrate, warning her that if ever she was taken up again, she would not get off so easily, let her go. Against Susie there was no charge, and so the two were allowed to leave together, the policeman telling them never to steal any more, or they would be sent to prison for a month.

"Susie never did steal," said Elfie, indignantly turning round upon the man as she spoke.

"Hush, Elfie, never mind," whispered Susie, who was anxious to get away now.

"But I shall mind. You never did steal in your life, and it's a shame to say you did," retorted Elfie.

"But don't you see I was with you, and so I mustn't mind what they say," replied Susie.

Elfie looked at her in silence for a minute or two, and when they had got out into the street, she burst into tears. "O Susie, you don't deserve to be called a thief," she sobbed.

Susie tried to soothe her, but explained that she was afraid people would think her one, if they remained together, and she did not alter.

"Oh, I will, I will," said Elfie; "I can't bear to think of you loving me, and God loving me, and being so wicked all the while. Susie, ask him to forgive me, and let me say 'our Father' when we go home," she added.

As soon as they reached their room, they went in and shut the door, and kneeled down and said the Lord's Prayer together; and then Susie prayed in simple words that God would forgive Elfie for the sake of Jesus Christ, and help her by his Holy Spirit to lead a new life—to be honest and truthful, and make them both love each other, and be patient, and gentle, and kind.

Elfie was still crying when Susie got up from her knees, and she did not lift her head for some time—not until the fire was blazing under the tea-kettle and Susie had begun to get the tea ready.

"Shall we go to school to-night?" asked Susie a little timidly, when Elfie drew near the table.

"To-night ain't Sunday," said Elfie.

"No; but they have school to-night, and it would help us both to learn a little more," said Susie in the same gentle tone.

"I don't know nothing," said Elfie with a sigh. Only a day or two before, she had told Susie she did not want to learn any more, and would not go to school.

"You'd like to learn to read, wouldn't you, Elfie?" said Susie; "and it'll be nice to go to school of a night, I think."

"Yes, I'll go," said Elfie; "they'll know me there, but you won't let 'em turn you agin' me, will you?" she added.

"They won't try, Elfie, when they know you're wanting to be a different girl," said Susie. "Come and have some tea now," she added, "and I'll tell you how I came to be in the street where you was took up."

Elfie had forgotten to ask about this in the fright and excitement. "How did you get there?" she asked now.

Susie thought for a minute or two, and then she said, "I think God sent me, Elfie."

"Perhaps he did," said Elfie, with drooping head, "for I'd made up my mind never to come back to you any more when the policeman took me. I thought it was all up then, and I might as well forget all you'd told me, for it only made me feel bad and miserable."

"Then God sent me to bring you home, Elfie; and I've got a place too, I think," said Susie joyfully.

"Got a place!" repeated Elfie.

"Yes; I'm to go every morning, and do all sorts of work, and learn to be a proper servant," said Susie.

"But you'll come back every night?" said Elfie.

"Oh yes, I shall come back every night," replied Susie. "I shouldn't like to leave you now."

"No, don't leave me," whispered Elfie. "I do want to love God, but I shall forget all about him if you go away, Susie."

"But you could go to school and learn about him there," said her companion.

"Yes, they'd teach about him, and be kind, I know, but it ain't like loving you," said Elfie. "I can believe about God's love now a little because of yours, but I never had any love before, and I don't want you to go away."

"And I don't want to go away," said Susie. "I mean to earn a lot of money. I shall get eighteen-pence for going out every morning; and then of an afternoon I can clean steps, and knives, and forks, at the other places."

"And I'll get some steps to do, and mind the baskets again," said Elfie.

"Oh yes, do; God will help you, I know," said Susie.

And her heart beat high with hope as she showed Elfie how to wash cups and saucers; for of this necessary accomplishment, Elfie was quite ignorant.

After these had been put away, and their faces washed, they set off for school; Elfie feeling rather shy at going there again, and Susie quite exultant at the thought of taking her.

"Elfleda! Have you come back again?" said the teacher in some surprise, when Elfie paused before the desk.

It was the first time Susie had ever heard Elfie's proper name, and she hardly knew who was addressed, until she heard her companion say, "Please, I'd like to come back, if you'll let me come with Susie."

The teacher glanced at Susie, wondering whether she would be as troublesome.

"Have you been here to school before?" she asked.

"Not on a week-day, ma'am, but I come on Sundays," said Susie.

"Well, you must try to come regularly, on week-day as well as on Sunday," said the teacher, looking at Susie. It was quite useless to speak to Elfie, she thought; she had tried her so many times before, and she did not expect she would come to school above once a week.

It was a little disappointment to Elfie that Susie was placed in a different class; but Susie whispered that she would soon be able to read, if she only tried to learn, and then they could be together. And with this hope in view, Elfie began that very evening, bending all her energies to master the difficulties of the alphabet—a task she had never even tried to conquer before, although she had had the book before her a good many times.

No one who had known Elfie, and the disturbance she made in the school a short time back, could fail to notice the difference in her now. And a few of her companions teased her about it, calling her a "little saint," and various other names, which Elfie did not take very quietly at first, and which would have led to a fight as soon as they got outside again, if Susie had not interfered. Poor Elfie had a great deal to learn. She could not understand at all, that getting into a passion was almost as bad as being dishonest; and she was half inclined to be cross with Susie for interfering.

But by degrees she grew more calm, as she listened to the story of Jesus' life of patient suffering; and before she went to sleep that night she said, "O Susie, I wish I could be like Jesus!"

"We must try to be like him," said Susie; "it's hard work sometimes, and we don't seem to get on a bit, but mother said we must never give up trying."

"You're trying, I know," said Elfie; "and I'll try too. I'll begin to-morrow."

"I think you have begun, Elfie," said Susie, kissing her; "and we'll help each other to keep on trying."

The next morning both girls were up early—Elfie to go to the market in search of any odd job she could get; and Susie to the grocer's, to know when she should begin her work there, for she made sure she should go.

She had not given a thought to the possibility of the man seeing her with Elfie and the policeman, and thinking them both alike dishonest. She had not seen him, and had forgotten all about going there in the excitement caused by Elfie's arrest; and so she started off without the least fear in her mind, but that she should be taken on trial at least.

When she reached the shop, the man said, "What do you want?" And did not seem to recognize her at first.

But when he lifted his head and saw who it was, he added, "You've come to see what you can pick up, I suppose."

"No, sir," answered Susie meekly; "the lady said I was to come to-day about the place."

"And do you think we'd have you?" asked the grocer in astonishment. "Well, you must have a good stock of impudence, girl, to ask such a thing, and I saw you only yesterday as I did."

"Please, sir, I hadn't been stealing," said Susie with the tears in her eyes.

"And the other girl had not either, I suppose you'll tell me," said the grocer.

"Yes, sir, Elfie had," admitted Susie with a heightened colour; "but she's very sorry now, and won't do it again."

"She won't have the chance, I suppose, for some time," said the man; "they'll keep her in prison, I hope."

"She isn't in prison, sir," said Susie; "she's going to try and get some work in the market, for she wants to be honest."

"Well, there, you can go; I don't want to listen to your tales about a young thief," said the man.

"Oh, sir, won't you let me come and try to be your servant?" asked Susie anxiously.

"Well, if ever I heard such impudence as that!" exclaimed the grocer. "Do you think I'd have a thief to live in my house? Be off, or I'll send for the police to you and have you locked up, and you shan't get off so easily as the girl did yesterday."

Susie turned and went out of the shop with an almost breaking heart, and sitting down on a door-step near, she burst into tears. Her disappointment was the more keen and bitter because she had felt so sure of success; and when at last, chilled and benumbed with the cold, she turned back towards the main road, she had no heart to inquire anywhere else. Everybody would look upon her as a thief now, because she had been seen with Elfie and the policeman; and full of this thought, she turned into Fisher's Lane and went home.

At dinner-time, Elfie came back from the market to know how she had got on. She was not so surprised as Susie thought she would be, when she heard what had happened; but she hung her head with a sense of shame she had never felt before, when Susie told her how it was they would not even give her a trial.

"It's my fault," said Elfie. "O Susie, what shall I do?" And then she burst into tears.

"There, don't cry; it ain't worth crying about," said Susie, trying to speak cheerfully. "I will go out again presently, and perhaps somebody else will give me a trial."

"But they'll think you're a thief because you go with me," said Elfie sadly.

"Never mind, as long as I am not one really. God knows we are trying to be honest, and other people will be sure to know it too by-and-by. — What have you been doing, Elfie?" she asked, by way of turning the conversation.

Elfie's face brightened. She had been very successful at the market this morning, and had earned sixpence, besides having a lapful of potatoes and turnips given to her. "I didn't take one of them, Susie," she said, "and I've promised the man I'll never touch his things again; and he says he'll give me a job now and then, if I keep honest."

"And you will, Elfie, even if the work don't come always?" said Susie, speaking very earnestly.

"I'll try, Susie; I will try," said Elfie.

"And pray too; you must not forget that. God will help you if you ask him," said Susie.

Two meals a day were all the girls could afford; and so it was arranged that the potatoes and turnips should be boiled for tea, to save buying bread. Susie knew how to cook them, for she had seen her mother do so many times, and she promised to have them all ready by the time Elfie came home; for she was going out again to try and get something else to do.

After she was gone, the tears came into Susie's eyes again. Somehow it seemed that she was bearing the punishment of Elfie's wrong-doing, while Elfie herself was more than successful in her feeble attempts to be honest. It was hardly fair, she thought, and for a few minutes her tears flowed fast; but gradually there came into her mind some words of her mother's, about the work God intended her to do in the world, and she thought that this was the way He intended her to help Elfie, perhaps; and that thought made her more calm.

At tea-time, when Elfie came in, cold, hungry, tired, and rather cross, Susie was as cheerful and gentle as ever. She had asked God to help her to love Elfie "through evil report," and be patient with her, and he had answered her prayer. And it was no seeming cheerfulness, but real and heartfelt love, that she met her with now, as she threw herself on the floor in front of the fire.

"We shall have a dinner-tea to-day," she said, as she turned the potatoes and turnips out into a dish. "Come along, Elfie, and let us eat it while it's hot, and then we'll go to school."

"I'm tired, I don't want to go to school to-night," said Elfie crossly.

Susie did not take any notice of this, and before their meal was over Elfie began to look better tempered; and by the time the things were washed and put away, she was ready to go to school.

The teacher looked surprised to see her again so soon, and whispered some words of encouragement when she saw how earnestly she was trying to learn. It was not lost upon Elfie. It seemed to give her renewed courage and hope; and the other girls, seeing she was in earnest in her efforts, thought they might as well try too, and the whole class was more orderly in trying to follow Elfie's example.

This evening school was really pleasant to the poor neglected little street girl, and she overcame her habitual restlessness so far as to sit quietly on the form as long as it was necessary; a thing more difficult to accomplish than many might imagine. Elfie herself thought that as she had managed to do this, the victory over all her bad habits was gained; but she found she had been mistaken before long.

The next day she did not earn a single penny at the market, and Susie only earned twopence, although she was walking about all day; and when they returned home late in the afternoon, tired, cold, and hungry, and Susie said they could only have a piece of dry bread before they went to school, Elfie felt herself rather ill-used. She might have helped herself to some turnips quite easily in the morning, and that would have furnished them with a nice hot meal; but she had resisted the temptation, believing that she should get some work and be able to buy some.

But the work had not come, and they could only spend a penny of what Susie had earned, for the other was needed to make up the rent. They had got a week or two behind, in spite of all their efforts to keep it paid; and the landlord had said they must leave, if some were not ready on Monday. The next day was Saturday, and they hoped to earn some more; but they could not be sure of this.

And so it was with a sad heart they went to school that evening, and Elfie had a hard battle to fight with herself before she could sit still and give her attention to what was being taught.

CHAPTER VII
CONCLUSION

ELFIE had probably never heard the maxim, "Honesty is the best policy;" and if she had, she certainly would not have believed it. She knew how much, or rather how little, she could earn by fair work; knew, too, that some of her companions would laugh at her for trying to be honest; but she did not know how hard the struggle would be until she fairly tried it. It had been easy enough to slip into the habit of pilfering, but it was not so easy to break it off, when once it was commenced. Again and again did she wish that she had never taken the first wrong step, never formed the evil habit of taking what was not her own, and sometimes she feared she should never be able to break it off now.

Things grew worse and worse with the two girls as the winter advanced. Often they were without fire and without food, except the market refuse Elfie brought home. Susie had tried again and again to get a place such as the grocer's, but no one wanted a girl, it seemed, or at least no one wanted her. It must be that everybody believed her to be a thief, she thought; and Elfie thought so too, and that made her so bitter that she said one day, "I won't try to be honest any longer: everybody says I am a thief, and so I may as well be one; it's better to steal than to starve."

"O Elfie, don't say that!" exclaimed Susie. "We haven't starved yet, and we've managed to keep our home too, though we have had to sell some of the things."

Elfie looked round at the almost bare room. "It's no good trying any longer, Susie," she said; "there's such a lot of poor girls in London, God has forgot all about us two."

"No, he has not; I'm sure he has not," said Susie; "he is 'our Father,' and so he can't forget us."

"Well, he don't mean to help us then," said Elfie. "It's all my fault, I know; I was a thief, and that's why he won't have anything to do with me; I'm too bad, I know."

"You're not, Elfie. Jesus died to save sinners—real sinners like you and me, Elfie. He saved the thief on the cross, and said he should be with him in paradise; and he will save us—save us from our sins, as well as the punishment of them."

But Elfie shook her head. "I can't bear to see you hungry, Susie," she said with a choking sob; "and it's hard to see the potatoes and turnips there in the market, and hear the men say we are a set of little thieves, and sure to help ourselves, and then come away without taking one. You don't know how hard it is."

It was true enough. Even Susie did not know the full bitterness Elfie was daily enduring in her efforts to do right; but that the struggle was a hard one she fully understood, and she said, "Only Jesus knows just how hard it is, Elfie; but he won't let it be more than you can bear. He will send us some help soon. I'm sure he will; perhaps you'll be able to earn a lot of money to-day."

This hope, however, was doomed to disappointment, as it had been so many times before. Elfie came home with only a few bruised apples and a handful of dried crusts as the reward of her day's toil; and Susie made up her mind to speak to the teacher at the school that very night. She had often thought of doing this, but the fear lest she should say, as so many others had done, "I can't have anything to do with thieves," had made her shrink from telling even her how they were placed.

She told Elfie what she meant to do; but all hope had left Elfie now, and she paid little attention to what was said. She divided the apples and crusts between them, and had soon eaten her own share; but Susie's remained almost untouched, and she could not help looking longingly towards them.

Susie saw this, and pushed them towards her. "You eat 'em, Elfie—I can't," she said.

"Can't eat!" exclaimed Elfie, to whom such a thing seemed almost incredible.

"No, I'm not hungry, only sick," said Susie. And, unable to sit up any longer, she laid herself down on the bed. Elfie waited a minute or two, and then took the apple and crusts across to her; but Susie took no notice of her repeated entreaties to eat, and at last Elfie grew frightened. She put the apple down, and bent over the pale, inanimate face, and kissed the cold lips.

"O Susie, open your eyes, or speak to me!" she said, beginning to cry.

But there was only a faint moan in response to her pleadings, and she flew off to knock at the door of one of the other lodgers. But the woman was not at home, and Elfie ran downstairs and out into the street, taking the way towards the school as the only place of friendly refuge.

Just as she was turning a corner, panting and breathless, she ran against the teacher, which brought her to an abrupt standstill.

"You need not be in such a hurry to-night, Elfie; there's no school, you know."

Elfie had forgotten this; but for a minute or two she could not speak, but looked into the teacher's face.

"Don't you remember I told you there was to be a meeting of gentlemen to talk about getting a home or refuge for some of you poor children?" said the teacher.

Elfie nodded. "I know," she said; "but do come to Susie, teacher."

"To Susie! What is the matter with her?" asked the teacher.

"I don't know, but I think she is going to die." And Elfie's tears broke out afresh.

At the same moment the clergyman, on his way to the meeting at the Ragged School, stopped to speak to the teacher, and looked at Elfie.

"What is the matter, my child?" he asked.

"Susie's bad, sir; she can't eat the apple I've brought home for her."

"I am going to see what it is," said the teacher. "Susie Sanders is one of our best scholars."

"Where is your mother, my dear?" asked the clergyman.

"Susie's mother is dead, and I ain't got one," said Elfie.

"I think I will come with you, and see about these girls," said the minister; and he and the teacher followed Elfie to Fisher's Lane.

Poor Elfie was in a great fright, for it was quite dark, and they had no candle, and how the visitors were to find their way upstairs, she did not know. At the door she paused, and whispered, "We live at the top of the house, teacher, and we can't afford to buy candles."

The clergyman overheard the whisper, and put his hand into his pocket. "Here's sixpence, child; run and buy a candle and a box of lucifers."

Elfie darted off, but when she laid the money on the counter at the shop, she saw that instead of a sixpence the minister had given her a half-sovereign. What riches it seemed to her! How much she could buy with all this money! And instinctively her hand went over it as it lay on the counter.

A penny candle and a box of matches, she knew, cost three halfpence, and this taken from sixpence would leave fourpence halfpenny; and this she resolved to return to the minister, keeping the rest for herself. He had told her it was sixpence, so this theft would never be known; and she took the pile of silver and tied it up in a bit of rag, and hid it in her bosom as soon as she got outside the shop, and then ran back to where the minister and the teacher were waiting. The gentleman took the change, and the teacher lighted the candle and went on upstairs, followed by Elfie, who seemed suddenly to have forgotten her anxiety for Susie, and lingered behind.

In truth, Elfie dreaded to see that white face, with this money hidden in her bosom, and already began to wish she had not kept it, for it made her feel so miserable.

At length the little garret was reached, and there lay Susie, cold and insensible as Elfie had left her, with the dirty dry crusts and bruised apple lying by her side.

The gentleman uttered an exclamation of surprise as he looked round the room, while the teacher went across and raised poor Susie's head, glancing at the dry crusts as she did so. "Poor girl! She seems very ill. What has she had to eat to-day?" she asked, speaking to Elfie, who had flung herself on the floor at Susie's feet.

"Nothing," answered Elfie through her sobs; "she couldn't eat the crusts and apples I got."

"And is that all you have had?" asked the clergyman.

But instead of answering, Elfie buried her head in the bed-clothes, sobbing, "O Susie, Susie, do open your eyes and speak to me once more, and let me tell you all about this dreadful money. I won't keep it—I hate it," she added, passionately tugging at the bosom of her ragged frock, and at last dashing a little bundle to the floor.

The teacher had not paid much attention to what Elfie was saying, for the clergyman was speaking to her, asking what was to be done with Susie, who was evidently suffering from want and privation. The room was bitterly cold, and the first thing to be done was to send Elfie to buy some coals and wood; and then, when the fire was lighted, for some milk and a loaf of bread. While the teacher was lighting the fire, and the minister cutting some slices of bread from the loaf, Susie slowly opened her eyes and looked round her. Elfie saw the change, and the next moment was kneeling at her side.

"O Susie, Susie, I almost forgot; but Jesus saved me from being quite a thief again. As soon as ever I saw you, I remembered what you said, and threw the money down."

"Poor Elfie," said Susie in a whisper; and then becoming conscious of the fire and candle light, and the presence of others in the room, said in a frightened tone, "What is it, Elfie?"

But Elfie was pushed aside, and the teacher came forward with a little warm milk in a cup, and gave a few spoonfuls to Susie. The first was poured down her throat; but she took the rest eagerly, and then whispered, "More, please."

The minister could not bear to look at that pale, famished face, and turned away to crumble some of the bread into the milk, and urged Elfie to eat some. Elfie, however, could talk of nothing but money, it seemed; and so at length the minister said, "What is this you are talking about—what money have you stolen?"

"O sir, I didn't think about stealing when you sent me for the candle. I promised Susie I never would steal again; but when I saw what a lot of money there was, and you thought it was only sixpence, I took it, and here it is." And Elfie gave him the little pile of silver tied up in a piece of dirty rag.

It was some little time before the clergyman could fully understand the mistake he had made, and how he should make it was then a mystery to him. And by the time this was made somewhat clear to his mind, he was compelled to leave to attend the meeting; for it was very late now, and what he had seen made him more anxious than ever that a refuge should be established for the poor destitute children of this neighbourhood.

The minister had placed the money given back to him by Elfie in the hand of the teacher, to be expended for the benefit of the two girls; and after she had seen them both eat a basin of bread and milk, she questioned them upon their mode of living, and asked why they had never mentioned to her Susie's wish to get a place.

Both girls looked confused, and Susie said, "I was afraid, teacher."

"Afraid!" repeated the teacher.

"Yes, teacher; everybody said Susie was a thief," said Elfie with a little heightened colour. "She didn't deserve to be called a thief," she went on; "but I did. I often used to steal things, but I don't now; for I couldn't bear to think Susie should bear my punishment all for nothing."

"And so this is why you gave the money back to-night?" said the teacher.

Elfie nodded. "I couldn't help it," she said, "when I saw Susie; all she had said about our Father's love, and what the Lord Jesus had suffered to save me from my sins, came back to my mind, and I was obliged to throw the money down."

Susie had only dimly understood what she said before, but it was explained to her now; and likewise that she was not to attempt to go out the next day until her teacher had been to see her again. She was obliged to leave them now, and giving Susie some money to buy food for the next morning, she took her departure.

After she had gone, the two girls sat talking of all that had happened; but it was evident Elfie was greatly bowed down at the thought of her attempt to rob the minister.

"I shall never learn to be honest," she said; "for if I see anything I can take, I want it directly, and I seem to forget everything else."

"But Jesus has helped you to begin, Elfie, and he'll help you to keep on till you quite hate the sin," said Susie.

"I don't really like it now," said Elfie.

"Well, that is something, for you did love it once; you said so," replied Susie quickly. "Jesus has made you dislike it, and he will go on helping you."

"But I am so wicked, I shan't mind about his help, if I have to stay here for ever; and it's always so hard to keep honest."

This was just what the minister was saying to some gentlemen as they walked home together. Temptations were so strong, the battle of life so hard, for these poor little street children, that it was no wonder they grew up to be wicked men and women.

When he saw the teacher again, he heard of Susie's wish to learn to be a servant, and all she had told her concerning her mother, and he resolved to befriend her if he could. It would not be easy to persuade any one to take a girl without a character from such a place as Fisher's Lane, he knew; but he thought his wife would do so, and could find her some employment in helping the other servants, and a day or two afterwards, Susie heard that she was to go to the minister's house about this.

But, to the teacher's surprise, Susie burst into tears, and said—"Please, ma'am, could Elfie go instead of me?"

"Instead of you!" repeated her teacher. "Why, I thought you wanted to be a servant?"

"Yes, teacher, but so does Elfie; and—and I'm afraid Elfie would give up trying, if I was to go away."

"But I don't think Elfie would be able to do the work required," said the teacher.

Susie looked disappointed. "I'm very sorry," she said, "but I can't leave Elfie."

The teacher had thought, too, it would never do to leave the poor little friendless creature to herself; and believing there was already a great change effected in her character, she had determined to take charge of her. Elfie could run errands, and go to school with her all day, and by-and-by she would learn to do things about the house and make herself useful; and she told Susie of this plan now.

"Oh, thank you; then I shall be so glad to have this place!" said Susie joyfully; and she went at once to prepare herself for the walk.

It was settled that she should go as kitchen maid, as soon as some decent clothes could be made for her; and at the same time, Elfie would take up her abode with the teacher. They would still see each other, for Susie was to attend the Ragged School of an evening; and Elfie promised to go to church every Sunday, that she might sit by her, and hear from the lips of their kind friend truths which they, young as they were, had experienced; and this above all others—"Our Father's" love.

www.ingramcontent.com/pod-product-compliance
Lightning Source LLC
LaVergne TN
LVHW041438170726
843492LV00008B/2681